Adventure Holiday

David Greenslade's books include *Celtic Hot Tub* (a novel) and *Weak Eros* (poetry). He writes in Welsh and English, and his processional work *Lladd Nadroedd* was a celebration of European minority languages. He has collaborated with painters, film-makers and theatre companies, both within Wales and internationally.

Adventure Holiday

David Greenslade

Parthian
The Old Surgery
Napier Street
Cardigan
SA43 1ED

www.parthianbooks.co.uk

First published in 2007
© David Greenslade 2007
All Rights Reserved

ISBN 1-905762-26-7
        978-1905762-26-2

Cover image, Ted's Fortieth by William Brown
Cover design by Marc Jennings
Inner design by type@lloydrobson.com
Printed and bound by Dinefwr Press, Llandybïe, Wales

Published with the financial support of the Welsh
Books Council

British Library Cataloguing in Publication Data
A cataloguing record for this book is available from the
British Library

Adventure Holiday

Psycho bingeing
she called it,
accusing me of
warming up to it.
I followed
a summer
of camps –
skull breathing
in Pembroke,
lightning dance
near Sheffield,
deathwalk
in Glastonbury –
rolling on
the dewy
ground
when I
got home;
but nervous,
so nervous
because I was
standing
in the kitchen,
tweaking
the beard
of a startled
dragon –
and had nothing
useful or human
to say.

Deep play — Freudian camping — He misplaces a phantom —
Pounding his shoe — Of lace and girdles — An attempt at tracking.

No object safe from word kiss word attack word touch word
cut word cunning word wound word trust word bomb not
oranges not cities not kitchens not cacti not petticoats not
airports not bats not pancakes not buttons not thistles not
heat-wave not the dead not speakers not the fine rapturous
filigree of self cleansing actual fractal pterodactyl systems
not the gilded incense of washed feet proud mercenary
necromancer reptile aggressively boiling earth meat
precocious student bike thief bayonet light fingered dry
throat pallbearer skate boarding dropout jaw beak unpicking
the shallow ship cosmos from fresh discovered islands to
holes in your silhouette serge street sauntering coat pockets
unlacing gendered schoolteachers from trade talented
workmen to karaoke singers to brickies to skivvies to long
distance picnic walkers their make up wig rich rip off
eye-flutter mascara beg bowl crude mechanical magic card
trick magnificent tungsten clicking prosthetic voice box
their drone beat fizz quick elixir bubble dry ice bikini
invited bedroom their ox cart boundary hot soul torch
combustible compatible astro-cartography birthchart.

In love
and the back garden
a desert of bikes and mud.
Two lovers
rotting on a groundsheet.
The hard, clear drink
a furnace in my hand,

2

sun on my legs,
food abandoning my teeth,
the bottle's prism burning out
when I carry it indoors.
Walls lined with beer pulls,
soul signs –
apostrophes
in a cellar room
as cool as a family tomb.
Rain blown under the door
puddles foreign coins fallen
on the bluestone floor.
We survive, stealing
jeans from clotheslines.
Each star a glittering knife point
poking onto our bed
as shapeless
as a broken egg.

*He sleeps in the lab – Pastels or paint: a pseudo dilemma – Aporia
REM type haka – Digitalis, peyote and hemlock – Word lumps,
worries and woad – Running away from cover.*

Switch the digital teacup skirt flirt high rise easy target
alarm clock for your flintlock trip trigger biro pen your
skipping rope wave bounce notebook perpetual nomad
irresponsible butterfly abdomen kiss thief pickpocket
accurate melancholy meal coupon hunger crow gorging on
icicles on iron on borax on blood on beer on semen on
yesterday on mantra on fridge magnet on lurid science on
east west seaweed dancing sea lion dictionary thumb drifter

you conjuror of all the winged and tricky things they say pass
and still sing glass about you let's now crack it stink horn
sweet corn you pay I pay money exchange parking ticket
cinnamon cracker asthmatic fortune cookie crab leg crab
cake coat hanger pluck the shiny globe Christmas decoration
one reach squabble after another discount flatter flesh fresh
from the throw dice exhibition calendar its nightmare
crossroads caravan aircraft carrier red for pleasure green for
treasure frozen military desert destination that brings the
swelling measure of the present moment down to one thing
and one thing only its suffering plenty far out far flung
many not possible any recovery of what was childhood is
now an ever changing locked hinge tuberous steadily cut off
septicaemia phantom recall memory limb.

She made
shapes
that might have been dogs,
dancing pink figures,
blobs that
might have been
men or women;
diluting raw pigment
with turps –
spirit
on her clothes
on the lino
on the curtains
on the couch
and sleeping bag
she called a bed;

her favourite
colour
laced with chromium
and lead,
leeching into
every cigarette
she rolled,
sponging her brain
until, primed with resin,
poisoned
and dull,
the rotten caravan
she painted in
caught a match
from her stained
fingers
and, without
so much as a groan,
became a bomb
happy
to finish it
and explode.

He lets his magic tortoise go – Diminished by beech nuts –
A gambling mistake – Trouble with the subtle body – Hip mechanics –
Laughing at plenty – Shushing the rattle.

Stacked a column of box files hinge folders paint swabs pot
tubes nesting boxes dress dummies sheets of glass holiday
postcards lists of venues withered wreaths grape leaves
memory slips comments on arts hints on business televisions

ranked against it pushed into the dining room nudged to volunteer sign the trigger brought into this world with placenta body guards frontiers soft as milk battlements of lingerie streets ribboned with videos studded with pearls multiple personalities delightful sayings charming qualities funny proverbs vague regrets thatched cockpits spherical grunts bubble punches spick speckle raindrops and a dreadful temper lined up like dealer dominoes red ant playing cards black team beer mats wild numbers devil foxes in-laws family friends demons wet varnish capsized harbour boats office blinds with healthy sun-tanned gymnasium arms waving out mirage fins refuelling over ten thousand acres of cold open ocean sand satellite conquerors head butting chartist forum torment sword chopping lost-their-homes knock-knock-knock jokes shoes wandering away tantrums divorcing east from west left from right in from out leg from ladder.

Discrete,
invisible
to everyone
but me;
her brute
effect, feverish
impact. It's
no secret
the way she
penetrates
the ground
knows how
she cut the world

into a painted wake –
a footprint going.
My eyes
adore what
her quick
step brings –
a shadow
to disguise
a bigger road,
as if I
understood
where she came from,
where she's gone.

A sinister tableaux – The sound of paperwork – Someone else's
tape-recorder – Implied by tickets – Twisting the night away –
Colon vapours in the sky.

The welcoming committee grim sponsors knife insiders
shopkeepers beekeepers temple body guards we'll take you
every inch every metre every pole every rod perch and
chain every step every explosion of the way but you'll have
to get there by yourself do the talking for yourself write the
notebook pull the roots up for yourself light the fire press
the fabric rivet panels boil the water pump the tyres one
dull dirty airport limousine between them one darambuka
djembe drum one leopard skin one clay pipe one peaked cap
a local courier on or off his head depending which obituary
which economic model whose bed of roses he's waking from.

It's right
that shines from
each wrapped painting
is luminous;
stacked deep
against the wall –
the silver light
in their bright hold
on me.
I squeeze
and release
them –
her tape,
her nails,
staples,
bubble wrap.
Pop! Pop! Pop!
Poppled,
stippled,
shimmering,
cellular shrouds.
They
don't want me
as much
as I thought.
Her easel
is what I
cling to –
and they
aren't on
it.

*Magic balderdash – Tidal divorce – Virtuous forgetting and an
envious drone – The shorts of a golfer.*

In a panic in a huff in a flap in a hurry frozen solid in a strop
focussed together mind on the job making a fresh start
breathing in breathing out entertaining a team of doctors
today interpreters today taking part in tests for experimental
meat today using a chain rivet extractor repairing bikes down
at the gene pool magnifying stem cells today the team you're
a substitute for still has a chance as long as you get in the
game as long as you get on the field if only for a minute if
only for a moment at the white lined edge who'll get nob-
bled so that you can who'll be broken who'll be scythed from
behind and the pitch what is it you think it's made of
flowers but some intuited clumsy music some echo of a
downpipe stirring a tune you whistle from who knows where
makes you suspect these pretty shapes might be chestnut
spikes might be cluster bombs might be balls of mildewed
hallucinogenic earth worms who knows who cares chuck
them out pile them high blow them down sow the downs
speckle the hens spray the bullets it's time to plough the
forest map the sea count the syllables curl back to the
ammonites fold back to the trilobites their chuckle suddenly
intriguing.

Six weeks on the wagon
then a smoke
and a drink.
As skinny as I am
it made my stomach wobble.
I couldn't talk

9

couldn't sweat
couldn't walk
couldn't eat
laugh, sleep,
couldn't cry –
just dried up.
My flat underneath a card shop
my letters through *their* letterbox
so we had to get along.
But then the anorexic who ran the place
opened a letter of mine
for the second time.
Do that again and I'll torch the place.
She didn't believe me.
I'd always been so agreeable.
Her face changed
when I tore
a birthday card in half.
Only a matter of time
before she gets me out of there.

*He thinks of Brunel – The secret life of objects – Hitchhiking
away from Eros – Starbursts, sunbursts, wormholes and yang.*

Lightning in my eyes that's the second time I know what's
up ahead I wasn't even looking just being told where to go
where to aim where to march where to step I tried my best
learning parts counting votes until the trophies came home
stained starred and acceptable not gleaming illuminated
twice blinded forever a column an obelisk a shelter a
mounted head a single poppy dazzle a blindfold order to take

the cantilever cable-stayed anvil clouds closing over the target transporter bridge curved as though busted to work from a simple frame forced to flicker flash soar storm to flood rush flush to overwhelm and transfer all ramp approached power station west trumpet horn interchange east above the curl of my shot trig decoy limp flag thumped clouds like cob loaves all for thick wisteria funnelled down fir trees onto an idyllic cottage that's just in the way just a blot a scrunch a billiard speck even the century can go time bomb when that's a trick what next could loop and delicately prick outwit quick before eggs all hatch they're gone coo but I'm afraid degenerate dove heart a steel helmet asterisk enlists my blood thinned by too much sight at too hard a total too long a fraction too infinite an option too difficult a sum too repetitious a short step strategy too much participation in harsh alarms burned out lights withdraw the fighter guards sky's disposable fire lighters ignite my ploughshare curling for the monument an armistice flared for the stick horizon charred black with feather swans blasted with diplomatic windows cold anticipation shouldering fear waste firework rocket sound effect and most of everything attack.

I find your diary
and stare at it
with one complaint,
it isn't long enough.
You could
have written more.
Each scratch
word
doodle

dot
sign
forces me to
shake the page
where you scrawled
the last lines
of your life out.
Each date
sectioning your eyes
burns
like salt
in mine.

His nose against the window – Breath of fire –
What one lung might have said to the other – No reply.

Close up there's not much to be getting on with an empty
field without a single seed climbing into bed there's a little
to look back on one reel in the projector and the film has
only static prelims false starts until it's finished with chi
kung pat ups in the morning then blast off vocal techniques
such as sprays of bronchial snap exhale the new relentless
from what tradition effortlessly coughs saliva thick with
ashes chuckles one irritates the other fireproof bombproof
plagueproof archives exalted to one linoleum flip new
performance techniques from active listening word worms
finally rouse a muster and take the gatehouse mining
engineers steadily tunnel deep into the ruined city like a
single-minded millipede swordfish tic.

Under the trees
more trees,
under those
the uneven table
of our beer and bread.
I wish I were
brewing you
some steady
listening –
your head
hatched into songs
of pure flame.
Traditional flowers
were not the ones
I reached to find.
I wanted wild eyes
from unexpected fruit;
flesh, stone, stem and skin
curling to the blade.
I heard the shrug,
cold shells
combed into
a spine above
tightly knotted ground,
locked among roots
buttoned fit together
until sleep,
death,
flare and fire
riddled your husk
from mine.

His flat domestic memory – One night in Edinburgh – Paint thinner –
A delicate wet-wipe – Positive Sisyphus, negative reflections.

I pushed the trolley barked the postman clicked the mouse cooked the books swept the galley saw them all roll back to driving tests sack race in Sunday School down the snake directly to jail bounced by a six back into ludo purdah it wasn't hard labour that bothered me folding metals carrying the lion's cage hauling benches from marquee to truck dodging bullets answering phonecalls wiping the arse of someone else's child having it confirmed that towing the sun comes with a few nocturnal nebula perks a goblet of cool nectar silk cushions and a slow shampoo while I trudged downhill with exactly the same enthusiasm as up but being mocked being prodded reminded with a bark with a belt beat the best I did the best I offered the best I dreamed came with a whiplash splash a nail sharp jab verbal bite a sting stab punishment a disappearance love letter suicide note.

We were in love
and noticed
everything;
qualities
the other person
didn't have.
We danced –
pounding shop doorways
with the soft anvil
of our backsides;
one night
losing a shoe

14

where the audience
threw beer from gutters
pecked with rain.
The world changed.
We lived there
for as long
as we could.

Asian labyrinths – Some very helpful shandies – An appetite for wax –
Man with dandelion clocks – An unexpected supper – Broken ankles –
He bows to circumstances – A monkey checks him out.

You've lost your job lost your watch lost your socks lost your
mind lost your income lost your car lost the deeds to your
house lost your dignity your stomach is sick mind is sick
you're sick to death of organised religion your girlfriend is
kissing anything with lips she's got a job in the Temple of
Aphrodite there's a crack in the wall that only you can see
snow on the roof lava coming through the kitchen floor wood
lice the size of ponies lifting up the welcome mat there are
chickens living in your car and your teeth are made of sponge
your sugar is low beer flat toothpaste ransacked your garden
is always in the dark clay and lime crop out like ice from a
forgotten fridge your heart is weak lungs are dry brain a whirl
of wrong-sized clothing a twist of insects a crunch of low tide
oysters a fry of marooned sardines a crack of withered
thistles cowboy boots bald at the toe free at the heel robbed
of all their medals small headphones implant difficult
listening at the sides of your skull a joyful citizen hands you
an enormous corrugated microphone wet and hot from the
spit of other spinning singers you want to sleep in the wind

and rain you want to sleep on a pavement near your house
you want to be dragged from the club and put to bed next to
the starched white uniform of a busty television nurse you
want to be put down in the morning you want to blot a
turquoise letter soaked in metholated spirit here's a glass of
water to douse the early flames.

I saw a picture
of another country
and decided to go there.
When I arrived
I no longer resembled my passport photograph
and was taken to an airport room
for questioning.
My hotel – dark, hooped chairs, white tablecloths,
serving a combination of European and local food
had, despite their letter,
no record of my cheque.
A fence of spikes and ditches
bristled its razored combs
and, as playfully
as a crazed, well-groomed Pekinese
performing tricks,
crushed the flimsy hopes
that made me book my ticket.
After a dozen beers
a taxi driver offered me
a place to sleep. He
walked off with my suitcase.
I looked for my rucksack.
My expensive boots were gone.

Too grim to giggle – The scent of an armpit – First person maximiser –
Optimum despair.

Three children play in endless summertime their voices
never captured always free untaped unwritten for now but
we imagine remembering chattering laughter and at bed
time their simple starched question where is mother search-
ing she is searching but they can't find her as the city is
rebuilt he hears many kinds of rumours what she sells what
she does what she tells others how she smuggles drugs and
currency selling flowers babysitting cleaning he falls over her
body in the middle of the road not yet I can't come home yet
or ever I can't walk I can't chew my food anymore I can't
dress myself I use a catheter I work for them I teach soldiers
how to eat plants and animals they haven't seen before I
translate documents anniversary speeches city guides policies
instructions orders school books I deliver promises of blood
when you walk in the snow when you notice their eyebrows
when you pray at the table erase me from your litany of hope.

        In Nakhodka, when just saying
        it was enough to make me giggle
        I was loitering – a student
        in the wake of other artists' reputations,
        trying to sell my jacket and jeans.

        10:00 am, drinking root-beer
        from a street vendor's aluminium cup,
        I thought I heard a rouble fall. It was
        a street evangelist offering me a leaflet,
        quickly handing it over in the rain.

17

Drink the Blood of Christ.

Strange and pale – she stood alongside me
immovable and luminous in wool,
teeth pitching inward at a slight gradient,
mouth open as if about to sing,
eyes deprived of sun and fruit.

Drink the Blood.
Keep your denim.

That afternoon on a thin bed
too bright, too hot to sleep,
nothing in my stomach but vodka,
chemicals drifting from the cheap latrine,
I opened the shiny pamphlet and read it.

Peter the Apostle
receiving the grail from Christ
turned his face and winked at me.

Grooving with zombies – Ping pong with sheep skulls –
He can still get out – The attractions of a job – His fleece –
What happened to his waistline? – Exo, Endo and Limbo.

The foreground is a sepia rubble snapshot crackshot terrors
published table books a small bird in short trousers its face
as startled as an outraged bear women in woollen overcoats
hands up in the air stick them up the city a pillage of
tumbling bricks dark chimneys grim exultant soldiers lime
pits less than six feet from shadows they are about to kill at

the same as victim time on the other side liberated workers surround The Loving General's tank his face already invested on postage stamps on tinned meat rural pickles on headlines among the extreme he orders one ordinary execution before inventing nominal tortures of his own where he whispers he bleats where he barks he coos ears slammed deafened numbed smoothed and shaved cut back to the skull where he leans souls break walls buckle pillars dislodge spines slip and reasons flip flack flick jack knife rot doubt and crumble where he pauses seeds chill grains carbonate fizzle sizzle pop and alive it's happy to relax by boot by club by piano wire it's still fun where he sleeps dreams obey hides flay families they witness and steadily mince in an oilcloth paraffin kitchen dead matches on the windowsill glass and ice the windowpane no butter no beets underweight father bows his head his uniform a leather ghost a dead train clothes dirty flat crunching underfoot.

I needed a doctor
but all I had
in the room next door
was a Reiki maniac
advising me to sweat and fast.
I banged the wall
and asked for help.
That night
my body
a white colander
filled with mint, washed
from a steel, mottled tap
over a deep, square sink.

I remember poking
a village bonfire
with hazel sticks –
potatoes,
fine drizzle
glistening on my duffel coat.
He said his name was "Eagle".
"Eagle, bring me a glass of water."
He said,
"No one calls me Eagle anymore."

Fried eggs and onion lace – A problem with teabags – He is startled by a shovel – His sun sets from the Eastern Terrace – More uses for a coat hanger.

What the kitchen for a daydream makes possible makes legible eligible edible indelible desirable we stir in next we study to improve to follow on to conform from board to knife to shudder to shiver to garden to before to growl once the maitre d' tried to hit me with a small steel bowl but I dodged and the bowl slammed making a dimple in the metal counter we both laughed I took him out to wet the baby's head I shouldn't have said anything or thrown dust from the barn but it was the end of summer and in that pale light its spray was a show of sunbeamed silhouettes projected high up in the air now I'm dumb and distant my own kitchen is a scratch on a pane of glass the kick of a housefly's leg a bowl of thin broth noodles from a counter in the station.

I took a glowing
soft ball – elliptical,
a premature egg,
slippery and white,
and I pounded it
with all the inventive steel
of an old tool box.
It loved me.
It was hard for me
to love it back.
It was thirsty.
It was hard for me
to find the milk
that quenched its thirst.
When I slept
the glowing egg pulsed again.
I drank some sweat.
It slipped back,
smouldering,
underneath my sternum,
saying – really, you should
modernise
your weapons.

*The dilemmas of an introvert – Desert island risks – A memory with
dizzy spells – Magic balderdash again – Connected with nettles.*

Depends on what the tide gave up or gives away a short cut
through ferns down the dunes onto the wet beach when
mark my aim meant a real catch a true story a pint of milk a
box of potatoes the whiff of a badger a tray of change a game

of memories caging a lemon under foil pushing rosemary under the skin of a fowl drives the work pleases the chef smiles the diner throws pastry armour around sugar armagnac ice trays bus boys cigarette lighters credit slips futured grain ransomed criminals aided immigrants hoarded for and against a government of national unity planned famine squandered oil wasted fields zero sky tyres into sandals commutes all cooking smells and not an animal in sight deathday no long hearse big motor sings but uncle will walk wreath wraith question and talk hide in the pew peek in peek out niece and nephew emerge smiling small field small garden my dust their red hopscotch sizzle there.

The party I started
in one country
continues five
time zones away,
where the pavements
are different.
What some people
encouraged there
the police take
care of here.
Conjuring drinks,
I smash
a pint and
eat the glass,
accusing the last to leave
of the gleaming star
that guides them.
Why can't I keep

the pushy details
of divination
to myself?
What use is
a distant city
anchoring its
long tent spike
here? Lamed
by travel, I vault
from pub to pub,
landing on my backside
like a beggar
in a shrine.

Shamanic tantrums – The index of a frozen book – Reasons for being male – When stereotypes take acid – Spiders in the sink – He reflects on clover.

Bingeing in Lower Scorpio we snack on cat fur sip high octane sweat cupped at liquidation from the sharp watermark of an active volcano it's hot of course and our inflammable caviar quickly welds hats to foreheads seams to forearms thorns to wire and the expedition goes ahead from gallery to gallery staircase to staircase cramming in more until the stomach is a globular lava lamp complete with molten street photographer and shimmering ice cream cart what we want is locked in the withered lime green crown of common weeds frothed in a pint's diameter angry like tattooed dates cracking cranium exhibit inheritance at the top of an inflated receipt even the logo goes up in price I'm desperate for the immaculate and she's keen on practical glaciers

nothing better than a smart promenade from absinthe sugar
spoon to folk dancer's lace trimmed apron merrily offering
the peyote gourd we mourn ahead and keen at the wail wall
computer screen it all ends in phone calls adds up to a clutch
of red perfume blotched around the solar plexus.

The pitch
a flooded tray
of broken glass
underneath
a multi-storey
car park;
everyone
had thrown a bottle
on it.
We played soccer
barefoot.
The secret –
steady,
don't panic,
dance anyway.
One false move
meant slicing
the plinth
of your foot
into bacon.
The dare
trembled
from player to player
as we sat
staring at each other,

taking off
our shoes and socks.
It wasn't a game
for the sober,
the feeble,
or for wimps.

A note of triumph – Venomous sexuality – Wet dreams and dry solutions –
Language studies – Psycho tattoo – His boomerang does come back.

Hey this stuff really works I'm getting high on forbidden
fruit surrounded by reasonable obstacles such as primary
school bare feet and the flattened hood of an angry cobra
tastes good tastes even better chained at neck nipple and
ankle until an unexpected invitation to sing hymns to write
them to squeeze through the hole at the top of the tent
into permanent night where dreams and insomnia hold
their frosted foot bones like bedside lanterns on a desert
frontispiece never judge a book by its content I dyed my
hair I shaved my legs upgraded my toga I slaughtered my
landlord and pined for the shopping mall I occupied my
habitat I was patted on the head and was modestly extravagant
I vomited and grew six inches in the night I felt homesick
was bolder than a bat copulating in the daytime I was
miserable ecstatic sober feathered and delirious I was
awkward stretchered and subdued I admired myself in deep
waters and combed my hair with the fingernails of extremely
withdrawn fakirs I ordered mussels and chips I played
dominoes I polished the glass ceiling I cashed my traveller's
cheque I caught the next plane home.

I found
a place to sleep –
the back
of an estate car,
and went flaring off
until a spark
came crashing on the rocks –
bricks
marking the edge
of the pub car park,
thrown at the windscreen
by two boys
determined to wake me.
To what?
I didn't move.
Didn't move again
when they smashed
a brick
through the back window
then the sides,
nor when they dragged
me out.
Imagine what they did.
I didn't
feel
a thing.

A solemn premonition – He is reflected in a doorknob – Remedies and excess – Objects vanish from his field of vision – Yogic clamping – He is unfair to a tomato.

Sleep is a mighty hurricane good buoy a grinding dipping deep couch bull horn transcendental predators bobbing gurgling chariot sparrows dashing in paint across a clearing between the cedar trees their scale dry claw pink bill hook toes gripped on hide gore dung on the literal precision of sober dreams my self defence a black belt five rhythms every morning pull-ups after work routine language diverted no further than the sign map without lines chant without notes room without windows statement without conviction commas without nostrils wandering a skinny paisley shirt looking for fat experience settling for a seat at the edge of an event activity simply a kiss on the cheek of something rotting Father Time tucking into my cot his lucid mistress at the shadowy corner moving liquid things knife and fork around and while the senses interface with more than synonyms antonyms unionise into a blank.

I closed my fingers
on smoke and grass
it wouldn't
have been difficult.
Sitting on the rugby pitch,
in front of me –
a small stream
deep enough
to bury me,
enough

to wash my face in.
Now imagine I wasn't here.
With no-one
to cradle me,
I found a pillow
in the stream's small stones
but didn't die.   I
woke up cold and wet.
A boy poked
me with a stick.
I opened my eyes.
He went away.
I had a choice,
kiss the impossible
or stand and waddle
in my clothes.

*Sorbian snake incident – Visceral anima mundi – Goodbye interior life –
What's the use of laughter? – The plunge – He loses his deposit –
She forfeits everything – Ferryman's big night out.*

I saw a red glove in a yellow skip two dark defiant fingers
sticking up like conjoined Agincourt adders amputated
caduceus on a stiffened paintbrush the bruised maroon mule
ears of a shaved date-drugged novice bouncer lost in lumps
of cool psycho tattoo lounge debris the corrugated brachial
gums of rough molar cardboard boxes chewed mouth open with
plaster putty mortar sealing paste ragged fleece vermiculite
snapped board tea bags insulation foam stiffened dust
covers pop bottles cloudy silky deep plastic multibond and
turpentine flagons split neck to end into pied melted sweat

rich crystallising amethyst effect fire-surround cropped out from ransacked garage shelves flower pots two dark rubber masked finger figures with a third a broken fourth a dislocated thumb meant a hand an arm a shoulder a stowaway meant a body double-crumpled bog-burial snapshot booth-enfolded improbable bubble signal offered from not just any tribute dislocated deft hand begging for any last small change for the phone slot or asking for any last train on an empty windy local railway station but this specific oblong steel sarcophagus and hidden refugee this specifically twisted pressed down thrown out drawn and quartered minced ground quarried butchered remaindered mangled haphazardly stamped on stained bled drained damp moulded ripped gutted wind-dried rain-dyed sun-burned chiromantic spectre a once working glove now ruined sacked exiled out of work on its bike but not looking for a job signalling that The Lady Underneath can withhold the sword momentarily prompts a final whisper it would have been a pleasure it could have fitted you curious King whoever you are I'll never forget what or how it might have lasted I like it this much out of reach playing for the other side departing visitor goodbye used up forgotten disallowed struck off sent off cut off debris drop-kicking this lot forward I'm taking my shredded mutiny this army of drunken untrained ineffective busted thrashed keelhauled slap-whipped leaderless rejects as far as Styx quayside with me.

I know
I'm outside
when windows
fascinate me

so much
I have to look
into them.
It's death I see
turning its body
a lot like mine.
I might forget
but every glance
reminds
me how some
soft things
pickle
in their limits,
while some half-
dreamt, half-distorted,
eel-like shadows –
caught by windows –
slide through walls.

Junk food luau – Hacking the Queen in half – Unlucky expressionism –
Reeds at the edge of the world – His kind of lip balm.

Abrasive outsiders folk painters dragon owners fishnet
models vagrant failures mulberry scavengers cheap mindbenders
vicious princes idle shiners capricious cymbal buskers unpick
the knots of a dense nomadic saddle blanket as it hits the
sides of an ambling comical caravan lopsided dromedary
ornate silver gold caskets holding sticky pearls of hardened
rosewater ginger gum in her tightly gloved expressive hands
her laced up body half-veiled face her dancing albino
batwings age tarnish darken and melt toothless rag-taggle

moon-eyed street idiots unite sign up subscribe shade
match cooperate and organise outwit the Loop of Pompous
as steadily as radical space-age caustic soda bites into an
ancient u tube see a falling row of hand-made bone-hard
iridescent Red Sea abalone buttons along her inner
sleeves dozing during rehearsals an overworked meatless
undernourished storyteller waiting for her wake up kiss.

I was doing fine
sleeping indoors
my room cleaned
not by crystals or sage
but bleach and
a vacuum cleaner.
One night, every
memory of her
I thought
I'd disinfected
resurrected
by the attributes
of an icon
I'd forgotten.
Nostalgia –
its sepia
crusade
advancing
on the dormitory.

The cleavage of death – Cryptic wonderland – Clowns sacred and secular – Why he loves a good cephalopod – Technological textures.

Everyday she leaned a little closer ready to dive into the blue thumb palette pool fall from the white plane commit to clouds wanting to cross from words to skin sometimes so intensely retro she forgot to cook the codes and came out five minutes ahead of embroidered time safely clear of looking unbalanced well into the security of getting me to praise what she hadn't even done yet our costumed act changed for each new stage free without concerns letting stable mass rush to please the edges with dogs with children with new objects that didn't know how to work the old machine.

It's hard for some
to be sentimental
about human ammonia
but I am. I miss
the relentless stink of our sheets
the amniotic wrap
of sweat and orgasm
all the debris her feet
armpits, hair brought
into bed. Her fingers
found nowhere
they wanted to rest,
cruelly testing my nostrils
with long reports
from distant countries
and all the creatures
she loved there.

The inventor of the wedge – Bedouin tantalisers – Silicon origami –
Aphrodite and the fishermen – He rings a bell – Flight out of Taurus.

I broke a blade of grass and made it roar bass clef into treble
movement circle dances hillside of universal peace panicking
belly first before the hostile stethoscope well-paid slimfast
gymnasts sad about starting worse about ending hippy with
nail varnish I could and did unfold her like an origami bird
press out her wrinkles until they were never smooth again
she liked it that her perfect square experienced mine why
wouldn't I unfold her confirmed by sighs by kisses smoothing
our barriers lighting our lamp on needlework where the naked
never thought their nets could be snagged barbed to fall we
burned flared dared and whispered her nearby tinkling life
stank of remote adventure a mountain I still dream about
she darned skins in silence I had to wax my only wings to get
there.

We heard this story
about a tramp
two fields away
how he burst into flame
and they shoved
the hose
breech, nozzle and trigger
up inside him
and couldn't put him out –
a blue flame
consuming him.
All that water.
Even so,

33

he burned into a heap
of dry ash
a nuclear goodbye,
a mere belch
of the solar plexus.

Renewable energy – His experience in a well – Small coal and even
smaller footsteps – Reality sandwiches – He swallows a bandage
and vomits.

The king's entire body is made of silver maggots eating at his
innumerable putrid wounds new flesh replaces rotting as
easily as grass growing in a well-drained field the king moves
like a shimmering illusion of incense and swords he reads
like a choral chant dances in an empty hall like the chaotic
climax of a battle whose outcome is still uncertain this flow
of sharp liquid metal quickly passes laws slaughter and
defeat sets bridges indulges in explosions at the very edge of
empire it draws new plants measures the lengths of common
eels sponsors amber mines in stolen provinces kneels at the
rood screen of a remote cell pauses to frown into the font of
a heretic cult his crown is made of massaged thorns his belt
of worms he bestows experience receiving as he gives he
exists he shrinks he multiplies he is lonely following a day
walking in the woods sitting near the river he climbs into an
old stove burning fiercely and listens to the confession of a
kidnapped child he's kept the letter that should have meant
his death and the glove of the hand that wrote it for over
thirty years he needs another queen what are all these
hungry children doing here why are the hospitals full his
horse knows all the boundaries by heart and next year he'll

send the court without him mills deliver gold farms abuzz
with honey he could eat his country like a loaf of bread he
can sleep in any direction he can magnify a rabbit's heartbeat
he stares into the eagle's eye but he eats from a board with
no one to turn to no one to play soft man with no one to
crush him to flint him to cry on him as he sparks and
replenishes decisions with investment with gifts he's heard
about a fish in an ocean his ships have never sailed he's heard
about a treasure in a cave his men have never mentioned
he's heard that his orbit is around that of another and not the
sun around the earth how can he leave his being how can he
reach for what he knows is unobtainable the vermin eating
out his throat arms and guts make a new body as they turn
to parts they haven't eaten yet steadily consume the heart
replacing it it's from the heart he'll venture with sword and
with cross but they fall from his hands it's from the hands
he'll venture with nothing in them but the hands fall off it's
from his front his back his packed insides but none of them
can reach a ghost.

No garden,
a room that opens
onto an asthmatic
corridor
of heavy fire doors;
stairs so narrow
my nostrils sieve
the breath
of anyone who stops
to let me pass.
A wheezing elevator

sunk into the building
like a perished
resuscitation pipe.
I sit near
the lobby coffee machine
waiting for a newspaper
finished from eyes and hands,
the way stuff in a bin
fixed to a lamp post
by a corrugated strap
is forgotten and fresh.
Hungry enough
I gnaw at
the rotten and the raw,
living on crossword puzzles,
anagrams,
firedoors
wedged open
every eight rooms
down the corridor.

The problem with activity – Literary illness and virtual participation –
Inferior bedding – He finds a doormat – Out of the bivouac and
into the night.

Neglecting his magical exercises zap 'n yams the scorpion
electric charm bolt lightning the sac the pulse star jump the
move hot suck blood gaze Loki's fork jag inner cut cup twist
Thor's mighty swash breath of fire ivy cling ghost leap man
dive the flagellant cold scalp frost spots spinal spike a slight
mould accrues across rocket lichen high altitude wine fodder

crust leaves jelly yoghurt leak scrape ear burn ash trace spreading from the solar plexus his skin resembles a strangely tempting leftover clearly from far away as far as his mother's voice his sister his school friend his doctor neighbour dog based on hygiene common sense fear legend domestic science eyesight taste and decency a small cough reminds him barks from beneath the bin groans from inside the crypt cackles from the airy cages stick it in the bin kick it into touch amnesiac instead he posts it on the internet indexes it on all the harried search machine alternative hope rooms on every apple in the orchard every straw in the lagoon every hat at the wedding every flax seed in the wind a virtual display of a moment of whimsical terror a wafered confirmation a mountain ear blood cut a gamble a scattered dust chart a thousand toenails scratching at dormitory sheets there is remote delight far away eureka a little gold at the bottom of the pan a cottage in the forest a swollen quick grow palm tree in a county of sand a scrap book for quirks quarks quacks insignificant coins tea cards saliva samples holy oaks cervical smears pen friends high hopes phone numbers radio static letters of the alphabet and furiously asked questions a community of top shot digit dancers top notch tent poles grip fast fixers and squid.

One by one
steel steps
cold steel rails
lead to
my new door.
Soap or sweat,
rubbing my hands

on my own body
I remember you.
Mattress springs
like paving stones
of ice. Walls that
keep no secrets.
On all sides
a *tachyglossal* pack of
televisions. No
one hears me
turn the pages
of the book
I can't put down. Early
in the morning
when I wake –
everyone asleep,
half the televisions
on.

*Personal columns – Seven Pillocks of Wisdom – How to Lose Friends
and Avoid People – The Chilean desert – Where the helmets are –
A riot in the mountains – Network of froth.*

Describe me pursue me redeem me remember me lose me
gouge me like a dartboard single white male unfit unwholesome
uneducated unsuitable no sense of humour lost in other
people's issues likes mime time crime tv and language nights
in nights out of it language any language your language wild
language bad language charm charger team spoiler weed
killer word killer hairpuller gentle jocular amazing and yes
sex go to Blaenavon go to www. barmeybalmygerwyn.zigzag

zintantincanllanfairpwllgwyngych.co.uk stroke most likely
fix it heal it nurse it pay for it steal it exhaust it prevent me
from otters from others from ostlers from yogis from lullabies
from bullies from counsellors from merchant seamen from
oxygen and overhanging linden trees make contact scratch 'n
sniff the ointment is heavy the reward is a waste of great
price I'm cool I'm in orbit upturn your rainstick clash your
finger cymbals chop your chard at the far end of the phone
at the fixed root of the mobile.

No matter
how much
I twist and turn
I wake up bright
as a detonator.
No matter how often
I wake, the same dream
shakes me
like a bouncing bomb.
I'm cast in plaster
head to foot, falling
through an open door
hurled up from a cellar
filled with gritty clouds.
Down and up I go.
Waking. Sleeping.
Fresh as a firework.
No difference
between night and day.
In the morning
I need a cup of tea.

A drawer
slides out at me – warm
cutlery – puckered fuses
nuzzling my hands.

Mobility in chains – Stuck up a gum tree – Koala fashions –
Eucalyptus oilfield – His spectral downfall – Of auras and tar pits –
Pickled in tannin.

I worked a lot moved around sat very still converted stems to
ropes tin lids to miniature furniture kept figures in columns
stood in the rain bucked routine split rails visited colleagues
missed the train inhaled fumes flattened overalls chipped
my mandrel in the gums of a confused and miserable boss
not even a nap on Sundays now I roll white bread for pellets
and search for jobs I'll never get domestic Sisyphus
sometimes I look down sometimes look back dance arms in
smoke around my shoulders see flowing gravel feel the
clouds around my chin another time counting my change
for a canned soft drink aware of my beard and what its
contribution is evasive cunning mincing suspicious walking
with a stoop then it's slippers or a martyr's life worth less
than a barrel of oil carrying an exile's rucksack a grey gaggle
of serfs all of them heavy on cardboard roller-skates creaking
across the rainbow bridge just in time to wash their hands
and eat.

Tom told me this when
we were waiting in the ruby footlights
of the shuddering coke machine.

Singh was alright, Tom said.
He didn't drink
but he would buy a round,
and even on bubbly water
he was crazy company.

One night he bought
two beers
and brought them
over to our table.
Here's your drinks
you cheap bastards.

He wasn't even sitting
with us. Anyway who'd touch
a drink from a bloke like that?
We didn't look at them.

Next thing, Singh comes back,
takes the pints
and pours them into my mate's
plastic bag full of clean laundry.

Then a blonde appears – not stunning,
a bit plain; young and perky.
Singh wants to see us upstairs.

He only moved out of the hostel a month ago.

In a back room
there's our old mate Singh

sitting with three other blokes –
all wearing ties,
all staring at us.

On a chair, next to where Blondie stands,
there's an open carrier bag
filled with money
banded in thick wads.

Look chaps, says Singh
I don't want any trouble,
just drink your bloody beer
and go.

He only moved out of the hostel a month ago.

*When banisters say no – What butterflies really think – Could he be
a lepidopterist? – His toxic whimsy – Overtone metalwork –
Chicken wings in flight.*

Where does the alert soul initiate its pass mark like a tar scar
on the shimmering runway too many chicken heavy passengers
on an overcrowded flight who knows where my suitcase is
pilot asleep the plane a joke me a caricature pausing for a
smoke between dreams no stopping when awake all because
I bowed to a few wild pleasures forgetting how it might be
how it might have gone voice implodes deep dark thymus
chakra exhausting itself in extremes and no great breast
arriving to adopt the world swoop lurch shudder and awake I
still have a lot to give I say as we take another dive glad to be
alive cheering louder faster the steeper we descend.

I was retrieving
a small elastic band
from the heap of dishes
on my draining board
when I saw it again;
a little bit rising
from the tips
of the ring and index fingers
of my right hand.
I was definitely smouldering.
I went to the bathroom mirror
and saw smoke coming from
my right elbow, a trace
of it around my shoulders.
Urine – pale brown.
I check the bed – scorched.
Check my shoes – they smell of ash.

Lonely freedoms – Nuptual sci-fi – Solar corsage – His decision to fantasize – A disappointing insight – When tents go booming – Pop!

Welcome Commander these surfaces are clean do you have the Tablets of Destiny and other things to do no my Twin is afloat and we must be vigilant we must be antiseptically clean we must be thoroughly well polished centrally and peripherally a salad centrifuge a venison paddock one table ahead of the enemy focussed brief hair combed spit polished must we be buttonholed could we be fruitless should we be worried padding our jackets stitching our trainers marking our homework red columns in ink between tense budgets in pencil we should be winding alarm clocks we could be taking a nap Welcome Commander may the Erudite escort you they are over all that disappointment stuff they're used up they've moved out and they've bought elastic no bring me Amnesiac Five I need her powers her money her leggings her athletics her singlet her deodorant her smile her teeth persuasion her abdominal limits her wine peanuts her aquatic tension and her bubbles more than ever.

Euphoria
in my upper arms;
nothing is a problem.
I fall asleep,
wake up running,
nothing on my mind.
I crackle like an iron filing,
walk like a bishop
on a golf course,
shot after shot goes
exactly where I aim it,
all I have to do is breathe.
The world is one big kiss.
But
suddenly, the angel following me
breaks its wishbone and
has what looks like contagious
fowl pest of the head.

Arson in the meridians – A fly in the zendo – Hit or bliss –
Ladies tear up your petticoats! – Leave your wife and marry me!
His kind of chaos – He sleeps.

Everybody turn to page one one six the diagram is a collection
of loose dots darker at the press of five fingers at the heat of
a bad news heart attack but this is just a faint she's fainted
he's brought the news by haversack don't call anyone seal the
windows I can deal with this I am a trained first aider dot a
cluster of dots an intense heap of dots a dot like you've never
joined dots before Welcome Caped Section Commander do
you find the fire extinguisher congenial Captain your knee is
on the lino the other is foreshortened into art history zap
while you're at it she has the 1950's in her kitchen I became
a Commander via Dream Exile I was a long time a Michelin
tyre then an amber bead then a sinister soundtrack from the
bushes of the usual line of carriages waiting outside the
Valentine's Ball I was a working glove later a small spider
surfing furze in Wessex having returned these are my orders
withdraw all data privileges our nation's history is in those
molecules sir reprogram your bikini young lady move like a
cat open fire The End.

This happened to me –
coffee,
the great anaesthetic,
I took a dose
rich as an aphrodisiac, then
had to take a big diuretic pee
behind the bookies;
urine the size
and shape of a man.

Then I dropped my fag in it.
Whwff!
Flames shooting
from my fingers,
ears already singed,
whiskers crisp
along my cheeks.
My pee went up
in blue flame.
Daniel
in the horses'
den, floating
through the betting shop
unharmed,
inflamed,
disconnected.

*Drowsy thunder and sharp reminders – Slowly raising an extension
ladder – The freedom to faint – Dozing in a rocket – Grey does not
suit you – Eating unfamiliar flowers – Then he farts.*

Coherent I'm not but gamble whatever it takes to risk the
damage it wasn't the least I could ask but got a full pelt five
pence fair price fur hat for one side of it go into the village
go on ahead as if you're angry or hungry or lost some money
yes it's not a game or role play or acting out either just follow
the instructions inside your plastic folder it all stays fresh in
water with enough you've learned I've learned a lot I've
memorised it all with unlikely images each sage and his
memory theatre his native landscape his local walk it could
be a natural history museum where the largest sea turtle

roosts next to the smallest bird it's an old problem a real dilemma and now the entire faculty's committed to finishing the catalogue before the donor dies scouring his shoe boxes match boxes caddies biscuit tins throwing out cotton reels cleansing an entire population of blind bandit musician marionettes from the painted backdrop hills.

No one wanted
to wear their crown;
happy enough
to pull crackers
read the jokes
fool about with
the squirty ring,
curly passion fish,
but no one
wanted to wear a crown.
Even when persuaded to –
by the end of dinner
red, blue, yellow, orange –
they found their way
into the bin,
folded into pockets,
crumpled in a ball
under the table.
I took my paper crown
and stole myself
a happy coronation
in the toilet mirror,
when I thought
no one else was looking.

Thespian tortillas – Hera & her insides out – Camping on a journey –
Mentors and card games – Remote medicine – The meaning of thirst –
His way of saying grace.

Forgive the tights routine good listening friends doublets
and cricket pads the repetition reception the comic strain
after flatulent onomatopoeia the sinuous stir to a different
mamba movement to lifting a beer before cheering to
noting a cautionary limit on playing with ladders in winter
greenhouses each action's frozen chant a green light flickering
for wonder but a lamp red dead set against breaking out
camping the tent flaps like a joke that won't shape into a
punchline a food melt that won't bubble at its amoeba
circumference a Christmas hazel nut that weaves its way
down into potholes of a family settee the warm inside chimney
breast admits sprouting weeds on its wet outside chimney
pot chained dignitaries stare into their billy cans while
beards grab for beans like eager crabs we sit together on logs
furs stones hoping for a cardinal direction as soon as I show
my hand to you yours translates my many eager signs into
one inaccurate narrow arrow function a part of just a little
gesture I never got around to we gazed late into the fire light
loose and scented roots stems leaves twigs boil up the
leaking kettle each hiss a cold pinch on all sides of our lips
my hands are suddenly transparent waves of krill bobbing in
the bivouac deep I jig some hocus pocus above the tea you're
convinced we shouldn't drink.

He pushed me under
the water
which turned out
not to be water after all
but a frothed
umbilical bath
of egg whites.
I was sinking
on an undigested
pea.
Who was this chap?
And this benign giantess
who suddenly replaces him –
washing her moonlit face
in birthslime above me?
When the immense couple
noticed, they paused –
and diligently rinsed me off,
whispering, while I, choked
by the caustic pressure of their hands
into a whirlpool of luminous burns,
coughed myself inside out.
"We can't help you.
  Find a magic spider,
  get it on your side.
  You'll need a team
  of extremely daring freaks
  to get you
  out of this much trouble.
  Over!"

Duplicated – A fascinating windsock – Bulbous pixies –
He throws a bean bag – A glimpse of infinity.

There could be many more of me there could be a dozen
extra a host a multitude an epidemic doubling hordes out
of the football ground onto the hockey field scouring packs
in town pick-pocketing by the fallen swarm onto the grass
in leaves squandered in the restaurant sending out
tongues throats stomachs just to cram more in at the shops
multiplied extra with extra elvish selves hauling it to the
taxi fleet anchored pennants cheering offshore how much
else could be whatever this pod of frog spawn is each globe
carrying a shrine believing that right activity might log
and excite it a dream of being next subdivided unharmed
but multiplied would be all I wanted determined to
increase until a new one gets it right from a cube of parallel
mirrors.

The counsellor could bark
like a dog, make
all kinds of animal noises.
One day
she came bouncing in
and said,
"Let's go boundary riding
and drop this provisional
life!"
I said,
"What are you on?"
She said,
"The same as you mate,

you don't like that do you?"
She stuck her face
so close to mine
I could pluck
her short bleached
whiskers
with my teeth.
I could taste
her sharp
sorbitic breath.
She could have bitten
my swollen nose off.
I was afraid
of the things she said,
the way
she roared them.

Clerical modesty – Cellular melodies – He finally hits the road –
Bruised concepts – An alembic at the back of his mouth – One big if.

All I ordered was an hb pencil when it arrived by bubble wrap
by international freight express I flowed back confronted
barely moving barely responding and caught a fierce look lips
like holly eyes like ivy smelling the small pink eraser pressed
as far as Stubborn Puzzling when at a tense gymkhana just
before leaving the clutch went on my travel limit and I did
get to go wherever I liked zipped there nimbly by big bang
by turnstile I didn't need a dummy passport anymore but hit
the signpost with a terminal nod goodbye each deliberate
uvula dewdrop distilled at calibrated sentry duty by constant
rain looking for 'something' getting in trouble more feet

kicking a metal ball more legs running the track there could
be many extra if I claimed all these if more came back I'd
horse around to everything.

Shhh.
Quiet.
Is this
a morgue?
Or
am I
in the right
living room
after all?
Where the soul
sits down with the heart,
and my body flirts
with the bristling
spectrum
of its Kirlian
neighbour?

Not all the homeless inherit
and the first in line often find
the queue for bread
has suddenly changed direction.

Sitting in a common room
with flame-resistant blinds,
sprinklers,
pool table,
odour absorbing carpets,

double glazing
and a door
with fire-regulations
glued on it, the prize
might be difficult to carry.

Staying calm
becomes a finely sprung
permanently alert
shock absorber,
provoked into action
by the uneven tune-up
of daily chats
with a crazy counsellor.

Am I really
making progress?
Or am I plunging
towards the rocks?

Is it true? Life
in a rockpool
can be beautiful.

*Careering antics – A train ride through China – Ash in the watertank –
Confrontation with a noodle – Despair and punishment – Benign
Myrmidons – His synaesthetic business plan.*

One moment of plenty increased by lots of scarce a bench
vault snapped into the sky we used to eat locally fermenting
our yogurt singing songs over morning porridge grabbing

blubbery handfuls of barley cod and goat now the avocado chip shop boasts how it steams reconstituted nicotine into the lungs of Tiger Lily and the Water Chestnuts it's a small world tailored with aviation lanes gathering the oily overfed into a polite request for closeness bless my Christian soul these airplane seats get smaller every year would you mind if I rose up this silly plastic aluminum divider here between us yes I would I do mind I mind the fact you smell like a disinfected lavatory talk like a machine look like a slice of animated tripe and I'm not interested in how you feel then we are forced to watch a film about a sorcerer who never smiles but he can walk through many bullets every time he frowns the same music fills all our headphones as though this simple melody rearranges the world for him like an army of lentils rising up from the grass where a moment before they were scattered and lost the film is astonishing even children on the plane stop chattering when the sorcerer weakened by hunger and loss of blood has sex with his female enemy on an escalator it makes me want to have rough sex also and smoke and drink a lot then kill the bulky nylon stranger sitting next to me snoring like a satiated bacon belly pig instead I take out my paperwork and focus on the next few days where I'll be with traders I've never met before there is a growing market for small tiaras carved from the renewable resource of domesticated boar tusks my speciality crowns for snakes I have a strategy neatly inked under curvy triumph lines drawn on bright blue graphs.

We had to clean
our own latrines,
a real *lle chwech*

54

they called it.
Then – one of those accidents
like dropping your books
in a pool of water
on the way to school –
a plastic dustpan
kicked
into the stinking hole.
Get it out.
We all refused,
gaping at the shit
like brainless fish.
Then the director himself,
wearing a suit,
tucks his tie in his shirt,
goes down
into a one arm press-up
above the wet dirt
and whips the dustpan out.
I bet it only cost fifty pence
at pound-stretcher.
He looked at us
like the apes we were
and didn't say a word
in English or in Welsh.
Then he said,
holding his hand away,
like it was holding
a sawdust mouse,
"It's just like washing dishes
  in the kitchen,
    someone's got to do it.
    Grow up."

Splitting an embryo – Midwinter spring – The squirming of others –
There must be an antidote – He refuses to gallop away.

Territorial rights one room in the house one chamber of the heart one fjord of the brain one side of the stairs one half of the school desk my share of the money double in advance with heavy millwheel bias when bread is baked with a shot of barracks charm with short sleeved beer brushed tobacco scented elbow invasion the popular universal self hasn't been very nice to its grossly convoluted comic body recently too much blood and shining one day too many pauses in the garden near the beehive near the compost heap the burial ground the honour sticks the chicken run taking a smoke on a sunny winter's morning too much sugar another day not enough between epicure manager cheering weary and puritan he doesn't recognise himself despite getting every unfolded opportunity a good long look tactic tactile recovery opinion options are mini-break tranquillisers surgery golf gold meditation a girlfriend prayer sarcasm comedy take a hike on the sick prudent dancing vivid dreaming late-night agony help lines a china a butty a partner a care in the world.

These were my pleasures:
opening a new quarter of tobacco
and melting the ribbon of clear film;
throwing the remains
of a cold cup of tea
with a careless cast
like a liquid frisbee
over a bed of chippings.
Imagine, set with sheets

dried on a clothesline,
we had a bed and
after staggering to the kitchen
coming back to find
you'd stolen my warm half of it.
We might open
a vacuum packed
ingot of Dutch coffee.
We might buy a rug
and watch the merchant
turn back each page
of a long woven book.
We might climb a gate
and share a picnic
where dippers burst,
sand martins glide,
from one side of the river
to the other.

He loosens tight clothing – What a plonker – Hirsute head wax –
It's time to be nice to his birthday – There's a place for us –
What vowels mean to a text book – He takes a voice class –
The sky is an ally.

Looser the better to be its own tent its own clean shirt its
own winding sheet its own silk parachute its own torn
petticoat its own red rag tied to the end of a breech of
reclaimed planks its own evening star millennial comet great
shudder deep sigh sea sign slough reef badland tow chain
towing nothing finding nothing sketch putting nothing on
the page pole suitor up there for a hundred days when he's

down she's off with a steadier man vow confirming least of all itself even the relaxed sub-animate sub-marine sub-vocal sub-sensual tense up rash out break cover dry cough chew lips grind teeth eat flakes gouge flesh pull hair break nails at shouts pinch punch first of the month a well-formed sentence mangled a speculative glance at the mid-winter stationary gnomon blade ambersand shifting style a crocodile caber toothpick snapped unplant from forward rolls quick bid chequered flag triple crown double somersault false start as minefields as fence spikes as razor wire as silent sabotage not as posies meadows spice herbs in leaf box stroll parade a gift of expectations of falling finding seeing how the loved world pie-fights in our faces in our hands in our letter boxes fertile eggs blown in parks trading estates alleyways football fields scratching their own Aeolian fun rooted mass forgets materials end chairs forget the border leaves boundary the heart-and-anchored hearth garlands to picnic sweat to wristband garrisons to monarch gaze to looking glass nostalgia's wistful envy living on nothing but a plate of common nettles tough as a dog condemned to the edge of the village.

I wanted to go home
but didn't want to abdicate,
I wanted to stay
the same with them
as I could be in the mirror.
They didn't want it either.
No one spoke, until
we found something
in the news

to talk about.
In the kitchen my
mother at the kettle,
me opposite my father
across a clean tablecloth,
bare except for a charity calendar.
I showed them my new passport.
On my birth certificate
his job – work I never
did. Then we looked
at photographs – all of us
sitting on the beach, proud
of my bucket and spade. My father
had five brothers. They
all could dig. They
even dug on holidays.
The beach an uncut cake,
always dark and fresh.
What we don't say
coos like a white dove
waiting at the door.

Simple pleasures – Ultimate lips – The dance of a housewife –
He marries his mother – He feels odd – His life is a tuck jump.

Half peppermints fall free of it cool merchants in fiery
turbans jugglers' scimitars conclusive flourishes light-hearted
companions discussing moiré textiles now they know there's
satin to be had almonds lodge there like replicated cuttlefish
in the bars of a warbler's cage squads of air punch down back
lanes like applied degree healing arts explosion rangers flinty

cinders brick tipsy columns a colourful card trick all the fun
of a glaring winter's day milk pudding tobacco chocolate
mutton and shampoo stiffen it the kitchen coconut mat
instant coffee bagged tea colour it wolf sweet sap sticky
beetle bright boot groovy we take a turn at shaking it &
beating it some henna their hands others keep a fag in their
mouths I try and follow the way we were shown the way
we welcomed the dusty cloud routine I'm delighted it's a
regular procedure.

> One morning
> we were sitting
> like a row of carvings
> watching a game of cricket,
> I stopped to redeem
> a badly rolled smoke
> burning along the skin.
> Wait,
> who
> is the king of this?
> Why is this army hard to stop?
> I pegged it,
> resolved
> and satisfied,
> falling down the snake
> ahead of me –
> quite
> content, that
> on from now
> until the last
> roll up – roll off –

the next throw,
the way I played,
would always
be mine.

Making sense of suffering – Keeping mum – The edge is the centre –
No one else's problem – He reaches the radio –
Thin paper and small print – He.

If it wasn't for penniless freedoms withdrawing our labour
and the right to challenge fate fare and destiny we'd all be
twin tumbling towers smacked by a remote outsider
someone hurt harmed singled out slighted offended
outraged blasphemed benighted sterilised condemned
annihilated flattened naïve thrifty pavement dwellers
thrown hands loose like innards into the bush detaching
amino acids from their food miles even as offal making the
safe world difficult for in-town bruisers kerbstone granite
cruisers impossible bouncers risky for around the clock hot
food radio television spear tyrants buckets of rice samples of
blood the right to gamble the right to buy a ticket to trust an
eraser so here's to the wretched and the meek here's to the
private language of blubbering mechanical hand-held string
puppeteers high precision missile sky jets rigged elections
walls in Gaza reassuring campfires white smoke jeep headlights
overseas military might cleavage of the dispossessed.

Summer
and the garden
I'd been given to dig
was green. The orchard
crayoned with apples.
Irises hoed in spring
flowered and gone.
I needed something
but I had to be patient.
The garden showed me
how to wait. One
morning I read bits
of the huge community noticeboard
and stepped under the eaves
of the shingle-roof
support and advice network
offered on it. Aids, drugs, rights, classes,
retreats, mental health, volunteering –
all with their own drawing pin at the top,
phone and e-mail number at the bottom.
One about a pilgrimage for gardeners.   I
dreamt of it that night, unfolding it
like half a treasure map, the other
half out there in the world
daring me to go.

A condemned man – His statement – Fractal reflections –
Skateboard & surfboard – Downhill on saliva – Questing for nectar.

I've carelessly thrown silver insulation boxes alert with
therapeutic mysteries connected location caravans to

generated supply built an island of smoke and mirrors in the middle of an empty potassium plain sleeping or sleepless a falling shape is an eternal ache once I might have yearned groaned prayed or rewritten or built a raft or set out SOS in driftwood cut back on fags or simply watched my diet all there is to reflect on now is numbing hatred of the mirror all it transfers like a fossilising cobbler how it became and stayed specifically this not some other reiterated cheeky chappy vagabonding else some generous restless wind with petiole lips from a forest of snowy silver birch trees leaves that wouldn't go away or execute a diamond finish just stroke the body with frosty kisses peck at all that's cosy with death's relentless itch.

                                   I loved
                                   her small boned
                                   flattery
                                   and would cross
                                   the city
                                   just to hear
                                   it. Sometimes
                                   she wouldn't say
                                   much, just
                                   "Thank you love."
                                   Or, "Haven't seen
                                     you for a while,
                                       where you been eh?"
                                   Asleep. Writing
                                   down my dreams.
                                   "I've been around."
                                   Skin like snow.

She had a mole
on her chin
the colour of a coffee bean.
"Helping your mates.
 I know you,
  you're a good boy."
I made a saint of a woman
at the post office. She
told me her name. She
even whispered where
she was from. Tehran.
She called me, "Silly".

Helpful allies – Bring me my sword – Chopping up mutton –
A whiff of mint.

Here's a red nose that'll get you through the joke a sheet
that'll get you through the folksong here's a marker pen to
get you through the lecture a light that'll get you through
the day here's a bandage that's better than any horoscope
here's a truth that'll deepen your hysteria here's a stone
that's better than a bed here's a forfeit that'll claim your
heart here's a breath for gilding phlegm here's a morgue
that'll contradict your cheering here's a pressure point for
clearer thinking here's a myth here's a moth here's a mustard
seed here's a plot here's a rabbit foot here's a pierced earlobe
here's a dog lead here's a hot bite here's a spoon in case of
seizures here's a skateboard for the royal road.

One glorious night
when every blade of grass
carried a hod of stars,
I wanted to sleep under a tulip tree.
I knew by morning the ground
would be white with frost
so I found some cardboard boxes,
taking my time, busting
them open like wedding
presents in the dark. All
night the cardboard shifted
underneath me like escalator plates.
My pillow, a pair of boots that wouldn't fold.
If I slept I don't remember.
There were other voices nearby. I woke
everytime I heard a peacock bray.
White scooped petals fell like gilded coracles
from the moon towards me. The city shimmered
like burning alcohol and I was happy
deep in the steady poem of my tree.
The wet park stained a boundary
around the island of my sleeping bag.

*Self help flick-books – Sleeping on an eagle's lip – One night in Tunis –
Occident by accident – A steadily twisted wick.*

On the mend bouncing back seeing straight praying hard
crusting over talking sense polishing armour bending rules
answering the phone making soup banging the gong testing
guide ropes taking a walk building a wall keeping a diary
making a dent in my drifting bed weaving sand renews it

perspiration audible as a bird brooding on a nest thump of
gardeners cheers it prayers and lullabies knees and palms
from beating it with gestures of despair from midnight starts
from nightmares baptise and scour it scourge it of days it
sways moves dreams from one park to the next reads by
starlight lift and dazzle it wrap its flight in a sodium puzzle
fire prism pillow soft dyed rolled out on sunset at dawn for
travelling compact as a folded thigh creased like a beech pod
mobile over saddle pads twirled in the tent it's pegged by
butter lamps by candle pins by blankets by human weight
until inhaled by sleep.

Black wax
and yellow
honey
the colour of flame –
better than chewing
gum, better than lager
better than
the last kisses
before she drank
the lot and died.
At the bottom of the hive –
legs, the dead
and the simply fallen
by wish, accident
and exhaustion. I chew
the cells they died in,
prizing deflated wax
from my teeth,
isolating my sticky hand

like a consecrated
novice. It didn't know
how to take wax and honey
from a bowl. Now
it does. Soon
I'll be an old hand at it. New-
comers with watery eyes
shakes, sweats, will
look at me with no idea
of all the sticky corners I've had
to hold, assault and sack.

The colour white – Middle C – Touching a cheek –
Nibbling at marjoram – Burnt roses – He buries a mothball.

From clover from hyacinth from mushroom from plum from
wet mat from water tank from patio feature from windowpane
from poppy head from honeycomb from broken flowerpot
from mid-air sunbeam from rain from shade when Mr Bee
prefers your skin he's married you he's parked on goosebumps
on body heat on syrup on buttons on fingernail on hair you
don't like him the lecher the boozer loser unloader tag along
performer God's gift to squeals to stamens to jampots to
pullovers and now to you he already has a wife a fat royal jolly
golden jelly one mould rich left over pudding potato flower
lava orgy geyser egg machine ceiling fan hand throb and she
has a thousand more she has a thousand husbands all of them
cruising until the final whisper she can hear or messengers
hear for her land queen promenade solstice mare parasol feet
washed by cowslip dew by peat distillery she's found she's
heard that he's discovered you and silently before very

obviously prefers your sweaty salt to the heavy clear glucose
she adores the ingots he beats lead melts down house bricks
scores hearth soot mantelshelves and pours until CCTV
drips cuffs interviews and blame until the sting deposit
touch and go leave a trace a birthday present a bullet leave
a scar a burning kiss near the wandering thistle rich border of
a blossoming hanging garden you were setting table cloths
and napkins raw food mashed beans rice artichokes tinned
fruit small pots forks tupperware bread cheese pop and jam
kneeling an almond tree among a dozen of your own and a
dozen more hang a halo on your neck rope a day around
your waist betrothed engaged committed hung up locked
in happy out of the parlour in the flowers in the world their
father your lover mechanic his trowel his coin collection
his secret life playing openly with pegs tents balls plates
frisbees playing with mud with aeroplanes unfolding refolding
lawn chairs sanding granite scalding marble packing millions
into one you're busy he's busy they're wild and fighting
rolling kites when this brutal insect suitor lands his sharp
charming spike in you cottager date rape eye voice glove
drop buzz off bigamist divorce this mad new monkey man
island hermit pickpocket purse unfolder you are not the
cider press he needs fling it off thud it with the fan of your
hand scream out loud injustice you who love dolphins pandas
and green your world with eco-products compact compost
conscious shopping rejecting food mile avocados Egyptian
potatoes radioactive celery for what bruised roots and muddy
greens the allotment market offers and now this bumblebee
fastening precisely on your busy thumb shake it off beat it
away ping-pong it over the grass no contact with the children
or the food you want to kill it but don't this bee has brothers
you gouge out its bulging sac pulsed poison with an angry
scratch.

When I fall in love
animals appear
at the very edge.
I follow them –
the birch-white spike
of a blue heron
waiting among reeds;
the yellow back
of a green woodpecker
cackling as it dips
across a field;
a black otter
shaking spray
like a fireworks display;
two kingfishers
burning through river
willows below the filthy
railway bridge.
I walk with unfenced,
untidy horses
near a basin of
flooded spear thistles,
learning phrases off by heart.
There was a fox
and, near Sand Lake (Ontario) a bear;
even the Babylonian track of an artichoke
when I reclaimed my oldest daughter.
Where my limits are indistinct,
fade and shine, I watch
dragonflies pincer
at the abdomen.

His magic tortoise returns – Conversation with a moth –
Larger than a past life – Flipping heaven, flipping heck –
All's well that bends well.

The world changes when I hear it call it light it say it weigh it need it from my lips close and changing it's a real day when Earth's my sober breath my word my eye when fields we walk are ours clouds ours and we theirs the hours theirs and houses where far way we walked talked paused and loved all ours I have seen a beautiful thing I have seen most clearly as she fell away and came towards me she turned her lightly violet cheek cool like a morning fig eaten lazily fresh from the tree reciting harvest verse as effortlessly as she held the rickety chair her comma'd nostrils exactly veined like fruit rolling dense with echo offer double helix glass laughter possibilities fine capillaries into an easy whale spout labyrinth promise spirit mound clear spinning reed flute plaited as naturally as baby's breath into the singing silence how she talked about my job that we could look at it another way.

A riff
through her shoulders,
only
a certain music
guides them,
until
wings
then paddles
unfurl
into a wheel

that won't stop
rocking for pears,
combing gravel,
probing
watercress,
and we plant
our dance
deep outside us,
having loved
and slept,
see-sawing her weight
and mine –
shine, dark
and –
in the middle of heat –
fine powdery frost.
It never melts,
it hardens into
crystal
fire
powering
the long dance
ahead.

Acknowledgements

Acknowledgements are due to the following: *Abbey News*, *East West Gallery*, *Poetry Salzburg Review*, *Poetry Wales*, *Roundy House*, *Shearsman*, *Skald*, *Unruly Sun*. Also Parthian's anthology *The Pterodactyl's Wing* (2003).